RESTING BITCH FACE

poems

TAYLOR BYAS

Soft Skull New York

First Soft Skull edition: 2025

Grateful acknowledgment is made to the following for permission to reprint materials: Alexis Pauline Gumbs, "What She Did Not Say," in *Spill: Scenes of Black Feminist Fugitivity.* Copyright © 2016 by Duke University Press. All rights reserved. Republished by permission of the copyright holder and the publisher. • Ama Codjoe, excerpt from "Posing Nude" in *Bluest Nude: Poems.* Copyright © 2022 by Ama Codjoe. Reprinted by permission of The Permissions Company, LLC, on behalf of Milkweed Editions. • Anne Carson, excerpt from *Autobiography of Red: A Novel in Verse.* Copyright © 1998 by Anne Carson. Used by permission of Alfred A. Knopf, an imprint of the Knopf Doubleday Publishing Group, a division of Penguin Random House, LLC. All rights reserved. • Ariana Benson, excerpt from *Black Pastoral* © 2023 by Ariana Benson. Used by permission of the University of Georgia Press.

Library of Congress Cataloging-in-Publication Data
Names: Byas, Taylor (Poet) author
Title: Resting bitch face : poems / Taylor Byas.
Other titles: Resting bitch face (Compilation)
Description: First Soft Skull edition. | New York : Soft Skull, 2025.
Identifiers: LCCN 2025004811 | ISBN 9781593767877 trade paperback | ISBN 9781593767884 ebook
Subjects: LCSH: African American girls—Poetry | African American women—Poetry | LCGFT: Poetry
Classification: LCC PS3602.Y33 R47 2025 | DDC 811/.6—dc23/eng/20250414
LC record available at https://lccn.loc.gov/2025004811

Cover design by Nicole Caputo
Cover photograph © Jacob Lund / Alamy Stock Photo
Book design by tracy danes
Interior images: TV set © dimbar76 / Adobe Stock;
static noise © Unleashed Design / Adobe Stock

Soft Skull Press
New York, NY
www.softskull.com

Printed in the United States of America

1 3 5 7 9 10 8 6 4 2

For women, for Black women,
for those who have been frozen under
the unwanted gaze of a man.

What is it like to be a woman / listening in the dark?

ANNE CARSON, Autobiography of Red

Maybe all I need / is to know men won't walk away from me clean.

ARIANA BENSON, Black Pastoral

Contents

Gesso

Dry Down

Signature

RESTING BITCH FACE

And So You Want a Poem

after Anita Scott Coleman

And so you slap it on the ass
at the bar, buy it a drink—between you
and the bartender, a double. And so the poem is
single, blowing steam after a hard
day at work, bleary-eyed and losing
hope in everything except what's in that
glass. And maybe you. And so the music
revs up and you drink your body into
a cage (two arms on either side
of the poem), enough room between the two
of you for Jesus and the list of tricks
you've mastered with your tongue. It's late
now and the rowdy Friday-night crowd spills
in from another bar, all mint
and maraschino mouths moving, marking
each other up. And so you can't hear
the poem, have to really lend
an ear to it, get down on its level. And so you ask
it if it wants to go somewhere
more quiet, back to your place. Once home,
you tell it to get comfortable and it asks
for a beer. And so you crack open two, tornado-
gulp yours to prove you are made
for pouring into. But the poem's not ready
for anything yet. And so you suggest going out
back, it's a nice night. And so you lead it
out into the yard, show it where you cut
wood for the fire. And so this is your shot.
And so you go topless in the moon's reflection,
nudging the poem to sit on the tree stump
with axe nicks that cross and uncross
themselves. *Let me show you how it's done*, as you weed
the axe from the earth. And so the poem

is impressed as you wind up, your body
more machine than muscle. You cut
a whistle into the air. The shawl of cicada
song dulls the thud of your axe bit
burrowing into the face of the tree. And so
the poem's two halves part like angry
lovers. So quick it couldn't scream. So you can't
begin to realize what you have done.

CANVAS

n. • /ˈkan-vəs/
a piece of cloth backed or framed as a surface
for a painting; the background, setting, or scope
of a historical or fictional account or narrative
                    —*Merriam-Webster Dictionary*

Textile manufacturers will bleach finished
canvases intended for painting in order to
remove natural colors from the fabric and
create a bright, white finish.

Essay on Shuttering

Nothing stills beneath your gaze unless you are a man with power. My father's looking made the rain of a storm rewind itself into the clouds, made it think twice of its havoc. My exboyfriend's camera: a handheld Medusa. How I hardened beneath it, and how he hardened with pleasure in response to my fear. The both of us shuttering ourselves against the other.

*

All little Black girls have been told to change for male company, have been aged with the knowledge of a man's wanting. What is comfort with a man mixed in? What were our bodies but a clean sheet of paper for others to inscribe their stories? In our own homes, we were inappropriate. When our father's friends came over, *Girl, go put some clothes on*. In the command, a father's knowledge that a man will always look.

*

Those old Easters, do you remember? We shined with hair grease. All us girls primped and pressed, dressed in lacy socks and skirts with crinolines to hold their shape. All of us: a smattering of overturned wine flutes in the pews. In church, our cleanliness was always mistaken for goodness, some currency in how docile we were when touched, pinched, inspected.

*

He who holds the camera has the say. The photographer says smile and I obey. He motions how he wants me to shift my body and my body follows. Under the bright studio lights of the photo shoot, I begin to sweat—my body's only rebellion.

*

My first trip to the museum was a lesson in etiquette, disguised: *Do not touch, keep your voice down.* My mother took me to admire the art but the art was too busy watching me. Rooms of pale faces, gold plaques in which I saw my reflection scarred by the names of white men. The women in the paintings did not smile. I gathered the courage to step up to *Girl with a Pearl Earring* as close as the black tape would let me. This imaginary woman stuck glancing over her shoulder, forced to meet every gaze she finds waiting.

*

Once, on a date in the Birmingham Museum of Art, my then boyfriend leaned in to squint at the details of a woman's breast. Said loudly, *Women were built so different back then.* A few paintings over, I gazed at a naked man, his flaccid penis on full display. I found no shame in his face. My boyfriend sidled up next to me. *You know, looking at all this shit reminds me that there are two types of people in this world. The watchers and "the watched."* Silent air quotes. Between us, his question fell unsaid: *Which one are you?*

*

I've never gotten used to living alone. I talk myself through jump scares in scary movies, make shutters of my fingers. Once, at night, I walked past the television and was startled by the motion captured in the glass. I didn't think I could cast a shadow with so little light. And yet there I was, a shapeless ghost blacker than the black of the sleeping screen. *Shit, it's just me*, I said, as if that soothed the fear. As if I could not haunt myself.

*

When I look at myself now, I'm really just straining to see who is on the other side of the glass. I take a selfie and the girl in the picture is not me. Some days I dance in the mirror and cannot catch her imitations—she's gotten too damn good at copying my moves.

"Asymmetrical Images/Curvature in Drawing, Especially in the Context of a Bodily Function Which Occurs Below the Belt, Tends to Conjure Thoughts of Mischief"

—@adamgarriereal on Twitter, in response to a
"Tampon Tax Abolished" image, 2021

Like a child, you call it what it could be
before it fully forms. I draw you a half-moon, you claim
a thigh that quivers in nosy moonlight. I sketch

the curve of a suture needle and your mind
will supple it, mollify the metal into a breast drooping
into a waiting hand. Anything cylindrical is off

the table. This practice of misnaming was once
a rite of passage, a multiple choice test bootlegged
on middle school bathroom stalls in nail polish

and Sharpies—the most sacred parts of ourselves
abstracted in our childish renderings. How much
mischief could a drawing conjure then, when the first

time seeing myself was not in glass but in too-
sharp angles and miscalculations, inches and inches
of space between what a boy could reach with a flick

of his tongue? In one sketch, the vagina yawned open
like a greedy newborn, in another, it bled
like a bullet wound. At home, I lay in bed, pried

myself open in front of a mirror to find the monster
I thought I was. Then, I tried to draw its curves and folds
from memory, tried to shade in where my skin

was darker than the rest of my body. It looked more
like a rose, mid-wilt, just beginning to stink
with its thirst. In its fullest form, I couldn't call it

sexy, it did not make me desire myself.
Like a flower in its last days, it only said *Look*
at me, look at me now. I will not always be this pretty.

The Day I Seized Was a Belt Buckle

See, it was me and my high school homegirls and lunchroom communion—
our heads bowed as we prayed over the boys finally filling out God's image.
Each week, a new sexual encounter turned chalice, a gemmed-up cup passed
around and sullied with our fruit-flavored glosses. We did this in memory
of the body and blood of Travis, DJ, Roy, of the orgasms my girls were just
learning to fake. If you read the Bible, you know that a woman's pleasure
is never the point of anything. I'll admit, I was jealous of the weekly tide
of unvirgining, a friend's new swagger after a boy mapped a route to her
counterfeit staccato in his twin bed. Wanted my own story to tell. So senior
year, I snuck a boy through the back door on a weekend night, wilted out of
my clothes. The dirge of my innocence benumbed by that carpet's softness. In
the dark I took hold of him. Unzipped my jaw. The reins of his undone belt
limp on either side of my face. See it was no longer about the story then. I
needed to feel the thrill of being told who I was. I let him lead me down to my
back, where I laid flat and open as a grassland in my own bed—green, fertile,
desirable enough to conquer, then name.

From the Photo Album

Through the aperture, a couch halved by sunlight. A soft lasering of light splitting the room in slanted twos. A girl is seated in the maw of sunken paisley, stretched across the path of the sun's blade. How appropriate, this early bisection/dissection of childhood. Outside the photo's frame, time begins again. Someone lures her gaze away from the lens's open-stuck eye, and she half smiles because she is expected to meet softness with more of it. Outside the frame, her mother watches the too-slow turn of her lips: *Baby, what's wrong?* The dark slit between her teeth, the corners of her mouth straining upward—a parody of love. Her school uniform small and crumpled with the afternoon, a boy's game of which she is early to playing. The smear of a greasy hand re-tucked into the skirt's waistband. *Baby, why you not smilin'?* The shadow of the dining room chandelier like an arthritic hand cast across the girl's neck; the threat a patient ghost in the home. *Go on now, smile.* The picture already taken by a man who says her name just like the boy did: danger sugared over with desire. The beginning of a confession lost in the shutter's crunch. The boy's name trapped in the aperture, in the apartment | "apart" meant distance between the "eye" that can see now and the "I" that couldn't | I am looking at a photograph of myself, dirtied with sepia. My eyes can see what I didn't know of my own becoming.

Joking About the Pandemic, a Friend Texts the Group Chat "I've Unhoed Myself"

considering Jason B. Crawford

Let us begin in the garden, hoe in hand,
the rusted scythe as urgent as archeology
(which only means it plans to take its time

with the killing). I draw back, dive the blade
into the packed earth until it gashes, makes
the ground beneath me uncertain. Let us

move then to my bedroom, where a man
makes himself too at home between my legs,
where I say *I think it's time for you to go* before

the going gets. *Stuck-up bitch*, swishes
with the sound of his arms sliding
into the leather sleeves of his biker jacket,

and I catch *nothing but a hoe anyways* as
he slips into the night, so let us
begin again with the definition. Urban Dictionary

says a hoe is *someone who lets any old color pencil
into their sharpener*; but who, then, has the power?
Who is sharpened by whose blade?

Oxford says to hoe is *to dig (earth) or thin out*
and this is closer to the truth, as men have lost
all the air in their lungs, have been emptied

beneath me. Let us return to the text message—
"I've unhoed myself" they say, meaning they
are the agent of the act, have robbed other men

of their spit. Here, let me translate—I've unhoed
myself → I've pulled myself from loose soil → I've
re-whittled the word as gauze to pack my wound.

They call the party the "set" because

it's cinematic how shit always goes down. During the pregame, the liquor lends you a lens, and every look becomes a slow pan, zoom in. Your homegirl bruises her new Revlon lipstick onto the neck of a bottle of Henny. Your mascara smudges under your eyes already, and why can't we just begin where we know the night will end? During the car ride, your girls make big plans for anonymous hands to shake something loose in them. Y'all pull up to an apartment complex and find the party; find the overflow—ten to fifteen men posted up on the outside walkway, calling first dibs on everything that stalks through. Inside, your group melts into the steam of body on body [chest to back to front to smack to hand to thigh to *my girlfriend don't have to know about you*]. Anything that sits still long enough becomes a seat. Some girls find their feet on the kitchen granite cool, pools of spilled jungle juice kicked into rain by their heels. A bottle, somewhere, shatters. One of your friends is disappearing down a frat boy's tobaccoed throat. You've got the word *no* pocketed for the cup a man will press to your lips. Somewhere, a bottle shatters someone. Find your corner for safety; the scene must play out. Watch and see how they all slip into their roles, how each frame makes a stranger of everyone.

Nikon COOLPIX S210

Once, I wanted a camera, another set of eyes
to magnify the small black semicolons marching up
the backyard gate. To see the ants the way
prey would see them moments before their feast. I wanted

to magnify the small black semicolons marching up
my legs—that dark prickling of first hair—the way my
prey would see them moments before their feast. I wanted
to know what it was to be a boy, I mean. To be close enough to really see

my legs, that dark prickling of first hair, the way my
hair curled into its own hieroglyphics between them.
To know what it was to be a boy, I mean to be close enough to really see,
took practice. I modeled. I studied the shots of my

hair curled into its own hieroglyphics. Between them,
accidental shots of my hand slurred into four. Getting it right
took practice. I modeled, I studied, the shots of my
body became clearer and less familiar at once. Everything felt

accidental. Shots of my hand slurred into four, getting it right
in the frame before the flash. I took nude photos. My
body became clearer and less familiar at once. Everything felt
like a distortion of what I could touch. I swear, I changed

in the frame. Before the flash, I took nude photos, my
brown skin ashing in the light. I realized the pictures were
like a distortion of what I could touch. I swear I changed
the lens. I still couldn't become myself.

Brown skin, ashing. In the light, I realized the pictures were
what a boy would make me into with his eyes,
the lens. I still couldn't become myself
once I wanted a camera. Another set of eyes.

L***, Annotated

The atmosphere of the bar was smoky, sexed
with cigars undressing from their tips. He fed
the jukebox, one song moaning into the next
before he eyed me, alone, perched on a red

stool in the corner. It's relevant to say
that I was looking good, was smelling good,
a *smokeshow* smoldering in the brush. The ashtray
beside me flashed with the foot of his Blackwood

as he tapped the ash into the glass. He turned
toward me, puffed the sickly stink at my ear—
this was his currency, a way to earn
my interest. I waited for the smoke to clear—

in his mouth, behind chapped lips, he held a new
thing[1] to unburden. He leaned in, puckered, blew.

1   I've called it *curl*, I've called it *wisp* and *waft*
like something a child maneuvers through the air.
Smoke is anything but aimless, got
aim, got game, got gall enough to stay in my hair

for days. I told my friends about that night,
the regular who blew in my face before
he spoke. I recounted the black-and-auburn light
dying between us as it fell onto the floor.

I remember thinking *please don't touch me* but
still feeling touched. I've been describing smoke
wrong all this time, been way too lenient with what
I thought I could cut through. Erase what you know

of it, I'm telling you, forget what you think—
after the night, my clothes ran black in the sink.

A Man Makes a Stoplight His Own Red-Light District

You'd say he rolled to a stop, but that ain't what it was—
maybe a sidle up beside, a pimp slide only that old Cadillac
could do, its rims still spinning like a record you might
fuck to. Girl, *don't look*. He's loud on purpose, got

the whole block's belly rumbling with everything
but hunger, that jittery bass like a hand around
your chin, pulling—*let me see you*. In the frame of your car
window, you are a portrait to hang over his head-

board, a brown Mona Lisa smirking as he touches
himself in the quarter flash of moonlight, a purchase
he ain't got the green for. In this warm summer night,
a refrain of propositions: *You got a man? We can't*

be friends? Can I take you out sometime? The watch and rings
on his hands, cutlery to carve you out that dress clean
as Sunday mornings. You got your corset of dread,
its tight laces. Can't breathe, but girl you look good

enough to follow home. You watch the eyes
of his headlights tail you, unblinking. You don't let air into
your lungs until he finally slinks down a side street. You are
impermanent, you remember. Your likeness, infinite.

Watch Right

Everything you do is for the approval of other men,
I tell my Black male friend after I watch him
change up his walk for a group of men. As they crowd
the corner store entrance, he makes himself into a bullet.

I tell my Black male friend (after I watch him
cry weeks later), *You are more man than those men at*
the corner store entrance. He makes himself into a bullet
to hurt something without hurting himself. When his mother died, he waited to

cry weeks later. *You are more man than those men, at*
the mercy of his emotions—his father's words. My friend never learned how
to hurt something without hurting himself. When his mother died, he waited to
thaw out as if too much cold couldn't spark an ache inside. At

the mercy of his emotions, his father's words, my friend never learned how
to heal. Or to love. How to let someone hold him as he
thawed out, as if too much cold couldn't spark. An ache inside, at
its best, spreads slowly—at its worst, refuses

to heal, or to love. How to let someone hold him as he
softened into something unrecognizable? Manhood, at
its best, spreads slowly, at its worst, refuses
everything (he does/has been) for the approval of other men.

Tea in the Museum

considering Cara Dees

We weren't your typical lovers of art, didn't know how to appreciate quietly. Perhaps this is why we hunted for each museum's ghost hours, where only a few other visitors praised the historic bodies in their somberness. No, we couldn't pause, lock-kneed, in front of each sculpture. We were terrible guests, snickering at a man while he pocketed and unpocketed his hands, at the quiet conversation he had with da Vinci's *Lady with an Ermine* about how he too wanted to be held. Oh, the way we ran the mazes, examined the fold-out maps and greased their boxy layouts from our pointing. *There*, we said. *Let's go there.* The stories we made up, the thoughts we projected on the canvases; the unhappy mothers and wives we diagnosed from the under-eye bags the painter emphasized. On a Sunday in the Cincinnati Art Museum, you stopped in front an Italian sculpture, *The Rape of a Sabine Woman*. Her hand reached toward a heaven that hadn't heard her, her abuser muscled, flexed, snaked around her torso. Both of them naked. The rest of our tour was silent. Later, I asked you what had stopped you there, what was it about that piece that left us both meeting our reflections in the museum's shining floors before we shuffled over them. *The fun of the game is in its possibilities. There was only one thing that man could have wanted.*

Sculpture Study #1

Brooklyn, NY

A woman's real first lesson about her body is nothing   to   write
home about. The second lesson, one of colonization. It happens in a big city,
the sidewalks gone half-dust and the woman believing   [for once]
there is something for her to claim. This complex ecosystem of space,
improvised measurements to guess by—the swing of a tote bag,
 a soft circumference of hair. The woman is eyeing her way to the J Train when
a man (made faceless by the crowd) grabs her ass. There are two options; be
crazy   or be quiet while the incident reworks the DNA.
[There is one option, because the silence sires some sort of madness later.]
                    Right there on the corner she stops, marbles against the
summer heat. Eases her hair from its rubber band to let *something*
                    free. The faceless man hurts her to still life, an inanimate
thing bedazzled in all the city's wet offerings [the day's earlier drizzle still
drying, the humid air relentless with stickiness]. What are we allowed to
really be when we hurt   in public: human or statue? As
if she thinks this into existence, the evening sun glosses her brown skin in a
coat of bronze and she grows   into   the   ground.
No one can tell the difference as they shuffle around her, give extra space.
Look how gentle they are
                            when there is no harm to be done.

A Woman to Woman with Mona

after Mona Lisa *by Leonardo da Vinci (1503–1519)*

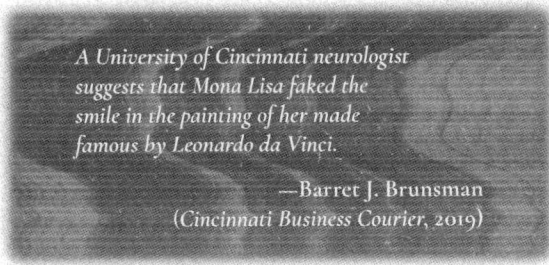

A University of Cincinnati neurologist
suggests that Mona Lisa faked the
smile in the painting of her made
famous by Leonardo da Vinci.

—Barret J. Brunsman
(Cincinnati Business Courier, 2019)

Being the muse isn't what it's all cracked up to be—who can tell us to freeze
and expect us to do it? Sitting still ain't no woman's work.

And Leo fucking bought it didn't he? Just swiveled his brush where white,
yellow, and brown made naked, said *sweetheart*
                                            (tesoro),
flattened the brush's hairs on your lips like a thumb (or tongue), an
extension of the fingers that could no longer distinguish between canvas or
shoulder. Thought that smile was his own special thing.

But girl I could call it from a mile away.

That's that *if you don't hurry the hell up* look,
that tip-of-the-tongue *bastard*, barely caught.
That's that *that last joke wasn't really that funny but I'll give you something*
                                                                something.
Trust me, I know it.
Ain't nothin' mysterious about annoyance.

But now that they know, let 'em know. Took them five hundred years to
figure out this was all side-eye. Girl please. I mean really,
                                        what is there to be afraid of?

Sculpture Study #2

Cincinnati, OH

Yet again, a woman hears the whistling of shame   at the bedroom
window. Past noon and the curtains still drawn. Everything unwashed and
stink-sweet with an unruly night's sweat.   [It's not what you think.]
Outside, the day simply goes on. A car alarm startles a sleeping newborn,
a Walmart bag splits from the sharp edge of a notebook cover and school
supplies scatter into grass. A mother nears her breaking   point
while talking her daughter through a tantrum—*it's okay honey, I love you,
it wasn't your fault* [over the small cemetery of color]. The sun takes on that
particular intensity, where it works into the contours of love and lessens
its patience. Inside, in the bedroom, a false   dark. The woman thinking of
the night before, when she asked a man [desperate] *how did you mean it when
you said you loved me?* Just then, the world a heavy   coat rended by an
old hook. An open   trauma, nylon yawning apart
under the weight. In the false dark, the woman is finally true   to her
heartbreak. This is not a poem about suicide, but she slits herself

          wide with feeling. There are ghosts and then there is   grief, both
asking permission to be cast out. The sun is setting, turning the particular
orange that makes dull things glitter. The curtains warm to the touch when
she opens them. Her tears, little found diamonds as she lets

                              the shame in.

Starved

Sometimes I go so long untouched, I start seeing things. Sometimes these ghosts show me new things about myself. Back in December, I watched an LA shop across the street hours after it had closed. A couple bustled past in the California chill and left their reflections in the storefront glass, where I swore they began slow dancing. Now, on a plane from Seattle to Chicago, I count the months, the mouthless minutes, the maulless math by which I calculate a survival—I'm not sharing the results. Outside this small cabin window, a wordless white over the mountains, except small patches where black crags slit through. Today I determine that my loneliness can soften anything, even that rock, where a dimpled thigh shows itself as if from a slit in a dress. I have people in Chicago, but no one I would hike up a gown for. I have a man in Cincinnati that I can't trust, that I wish I could, who touches the base of my neck when I least expect it. The last time, I startled beneath his palm, and he laughed at my horror.

The Ongoing Debate

after Girl in Bath, II (Petra) *by Eric Gill (1923)*

> *This was an envelope in the Ditchling archives, on the back of which, in two columns, Gill had listed, in some detail, the measurements of various parts of the bodies of his daughters, Elizabeth (Betty) and Petra. "Adjacent to those are his own measurements and then, at the bottom, he writes his penis size, erect and flaccid. It's a powerful object. It very quickly tells the story. You can't look at it and say: 'He was a sculptor, of course he was interested in measurements and form.'"*
>
> —Rachel Cooke interview with Nathaniel Hepburn, on the artist Eric Gill's sexual abuse of his daughters, and how it informed his art (*The Guardian*, 2017)

They always ask *Well can't we separate*
the abuser from the art? And yet the artist
marries his art with his darkness, serves it on a plate
of wood. What are these sketches but a harvest

of your crimes? Eric, she's folding into herself, her hair
her only protection. You make her woman, make
her object. You say *Look at my Petra*, share
her with other men like you, who cannot take

their eyes away from what tries to shut them out.
Before the bath, you took her *measurements*.
Petra, a standing crucifixion sprout-
ing goosebumps beneath your twisted reverence.

My goodness, Petra, look how much you've grown.
You graze a nipple, pubic hair; things she never owned.

They Say Chivalry Is Dead

Tonight, it's all precarious—the bottles
of vintage wine in their honeycomb racks, the waitress
who flushes as you order, our first date mottled
by hot-faced desire. You say, *I couldn't waste this*

one chance to get to know you. Months, you asked
to take me out and I stalled—every evening
I've given to a man could've been my last
bet on tomorrow. The waitress spills the riesling

in my lap 'cause she's distracted, darkens the dress-
gulch in between my thighs. You threaten to slash
her tip in half, and I should be impressed
at this chivalrous exchange—withholding your cash

for my honor. Here's the blueprint, the architecture
of my delusion—I'm *flattered.* Your lecture

on service services me. I want to take
you home right now. But the night begins to turn,
tilt on a violent axis. Make no mistake,
I owe you now. I've seen the TikToks, learned

a man will stand and watch another man
assault a woman in the street if he don't
own her. This bid for ownership, your plan
all along. The waitress returns ashamed, won't

look up from our cemetery of empty plates.
You offer your card. You pay for me—denuded,
deluded by a practiced kindness—place
your knee against mine. Yes, I've alluded

to the end. The billholder closes; guillotines
my fate. I dare not smile. I know what this means.

If I Marry a Poet, We Will Argue over Descriptions

In bed, before the frictioned hush of dry shins untangling, he sees the sun nosing through the window and begging at our feet. Asks me *Who is the better poet, I wonder?* He loves me because I humor him, because I tell him to put his money where every part of my body has been. He says *The sun waits for us at the foot of the bed like a pup waiting to be fed.* I say *The sun shadows out its own Morse code on the sheets, goads us to waking and wanting what we don't have time for.* He gets suggestive, says *We have time now,* but no no, I make him finish what he has started.

Frustrated, he says *The sun is an anvil of heat that beats the window to breaking.* I say *The sun is a pulley that pulls me from the worst dreams.* He says *The sun is surgical, surging through the gauze of clouds like scissors.* I say *The sun sutures what the dark split the night before.* And when we talk in opposites like this, he gets extreme. Calls the sun everything but a child of God—*Peeping Tom, blind motherfucker, that jealous, jealous gold.* Oh, how do I tell him? How do I tell him that he's shown me everything about him, everything he thought I'd never know?

When I Say No, the Joker Smiles

In the dark theater, I stale with the popcorn left
between the seats. My boyfriend's getting handsy.
Behind, a few rows up, a man observes the theft

of my growls as they slip from my swollen lips, bereft
of control or *no*. My boyfriend knows I can't see
in the dark theater. I stale with the popcorn left

between his teeth, his buttered and salted breath
panting a mist on my neck. He won't unhand me.
Behind, a few rows up, a man observes. The theft

happens, unnoticed by only a few. It's swept
under the rug. On screen, the Joker's dancing.
In the dark theater, I stale. With the popcorn left

on the ground, my boyfriend grinds his palm on the cleft
between my thighs. The Joker hollers like a banshee.
Behind, a few rows up, a man observes the theft

of my scream. The Joker paints a happy face, deft
with his finger movements. My boyfriend smiles at me
in the dark theater. I stale with the popcorn left
behind. A few rows up, a man observes the theft.

Lessons in Grief, Piedmont Triad International Airport (GSO), 5:06 AM

I hurt through the terminals. I blow out

> my eardrums with bass (to make parentheses of pain around my
> heartache). This early in the morning, the sky is a demiblue dark
> enough to muzzle

anything I'd smile at. At the gate, an apocalypse

> of exhaustion. When boarding begins, I stare at a black wire sculpture
> of a man sitting on the edge of a chair, his chin in his hand as he
> leans forward. A child unscrews

her hand from her mother's fist to run toward it (and I've written the end of
this scene

> in my mind already, where the child's curiosity guides her hand toward
> what she shouldn't

touch). She reaches the figure and stops, backs away, looks back at her
mother for help. Up close, the wire cold, the man uninviting. The little
girl is lucky like some children

> who learned early on about what could hurt them and how to

avoid it. She begins to cry and I've witnessed her first heartbreak (what it's
like to get up close to a man and see him clearly when

> it's too late). The girl's mother comes over, pulls her firmly away by
> the arm—

and is there a better way to be saved? The sculpture remains rapt with
attention, waiting for a conversation. I know the coldness

of men, have snaked my body around the wiry metal of the heartless, and still I find myself thinking of the statue,

how lonely a life. My friends say I am too empathetic, and this is why I struggle to walk away from who hurts me. *You see humanity where there is none,* one texts.

How lonely a life, I mouth to myself.

Photography

Somewhere, my body develops apart from me—
in a dark room, on a square of a Polaroid.

    In a dark room, on a square of a Polaroid,
        someone's pinched fingers pull me from the realm of ghost.

Someone's pinched fingers pull me from the realm of ghost;
a photographer snaps to grab my attention.

    A photographer snaps to grab my attention
        to the doe-eyed camera lens. *Look at me, honey!*

To the doe-eyed camera lens, look at me honey
in the flash. I'm only real if you capture me.

    In the flash, I'm only real if you capture me
        looking into the lens. You double behind it.

Looking into the lens, you double behind it.
Somewhere, my body develops apart from me.

GESSO

n. • /ˈje-sō/
a hard compound of plaster of Paris or whiting
in glue, used in sculpture or as a base for gilding
or painting on wood.

Gesso primes the surface for painting. It dries
hard, making the canvas stiffer, which allows
paint to be manipulated more easily on its
surface.

Water as Villain Origin Story

1.

Would you believe they blamed the river? For its
honesty, the way it forages for anything's likeness.
Bleeds each season's foliage from the trees then
suspends the leaves in its wet resin. When I say *they*, I
mean the gods. When I say *the gods*, I am refusing to
trouble the waters with my learning. History tells us
a German chemist discovered the modern-day mirror,
silvered glass like a rotted tooth. History traces back to
poorer models of copper and bronze, but does not find
its way back to the pre-speech technology of water.
What I mean is that myth and history are man-made,
both created to explain away their sins.

2.

The other day a man suggested rain was a myth, out in
the open. As we waited at the curb for an Uber, the sky
grumbled like a father trucked from slumber.
Somewhere, a small stream spidered out to a full split
before the nocturnal water broke. In the storm, he
jettied his arm from the body's marsh and opened his
palm. Asked *why can't I hold it?*, willing gravity to soften
with sympathy. I have to tell you that this was a date
and I didn't call him back. I have to tell you that it was
not irrationality that had him cupping the air, but envy,
and this brings me back to softening. The state of
things. The crescent of his hand, flexed into a gourd.
Water, going from vapor to liquid to looking glass.
Tucked into the chemistry of it, there is a joke about
men softening and hardening, I swear.

3.

In every tragic story about a woman, water is a parenthetical (a young girl watching the neighbor's son beat his own reflection in the lip of a murky pond, failing to rid himself of how much of his father he found in it; an older girl's scalding shower to wash away a tragic evidence; me, on that date, witnessing a man's ego rear its head in the storm). Even Medusa, raped by the god of the sea in Athena's temple. I won't rehash the details, but her killer had to seek out her reflection in a mirrored shield to behead her. By the gods' design, he watched himself do it. He was his own understudy.

4.

While doing dishes a while back, I cut my finger on a steak knife hidden beneath the quilted foam. Ran it under warm water, the bleeding as urgent as Poseidon's touch, or a man inviting himself into a woman's smile. The skin softened, and I know I'm supposed to say something about softening as sabotage but it isn't my place. Crying, I called out for my lover. He wrapped my hand in damp paper towels over the sink, tenderly applied pressure. When my first tear fell, he startled at the new moisture, looked fully into my eyes. Whatever he found in their surface—my pain, relief, the secret knowledge that the water from the sink would have been a gentler healer—turned him to stone.

Mirror Stage

In the mirror, I trouble my existence with another self. I have just learned of whole things and too soon do I learn of doubling. I cycle through fear and joy and back again with the knowledge that I can do what I want myself to do. I put a hand to the glass and I am cool where I know there's heat. I kiss myself and find me unwelcoming. I blow onto the glass and my second self does not receive my breath on my tongue. Decades later, I eye the I I've been straining to touch for years. I play games with me. I lean in and the self leans in. I step back and I step back. I press a finger to the glass and we point at ourselves. I split again, from two, to four, eight to more. Another eye, another I—another eye/I for me to answer to.

In a Picture on My Boyfriend's Phone

Another woman ripples,
naked in his eager grasp.
In our bed, they dirty the sheets
I cleaned. He snaps photos,
fills the memory card—
shot after shot
of a woman who looks like me.
I do not know
how to leave him.
I touch him, I learn
to step outside myself.
He makes love to a distant thing and records it.
To step outside myself,
I touch him. I learn
how to leave him.
I do not know
of a woman who looks like me.
Shot after shot
fills the memory card
I cleaned. He snaps photos
in our bed. They dirty the sheets.
Naked, in his eager grasp,
another woman ripples.

Investigation

could have colored my surprise, coming across a picture of me in the old apartment, young and flushed in the living room's floor-length mirror. my memory glitches in the shadow of this evidence; the couch i dream in green glares ruby in the reflection. our relationship emeralds in my remembering; a jade couch, the olive duvet, the forest pillowcase greened darker with tears. you hated green, never wore it. i bore it because it was my school color. here in the photograph: my black shirt, black jeans, the red, red couch. i would call to compare notes if there wasn't so much hate between us. *how would you remember it? how would you remember me?* in my head i can see you laugh in this greened-sepia film. i watch the bruise from my birth control implant green in the already viridian thought. the lie of the couch again. looking at this photo, i know nothing was ever green in that apartment, that we decorated in the Alabama crimson. i wave wet-mouthing my other memories shape. the couch is red in truth. god, is a red bruise name of the tide; know the truth is a the shore of how help this one take green in memory, how my memory disintegrating.

the traffic light was green, gone peaky in the storm. you were so angry with my sluggish forgiveness. you had the signal to go, both here on this street and elsewhere. you could have just left me, should have. the car behind us honks. i tell you, softly, to go. look at all this encouragement.

green trees blurred to one unending
    ribbon on the highway in
    Birmingham
green veins that verdant in certain light
green-eyed envy
green two-tones, the jade (?) suede
    cough fickle beneath my touch
green of your money
green of the money i didn't have
green rot of uneaten salad in the sink
green nausea
green bile i hook from my throat

green bewilderment
at the end of a
deep bruise. some
colors are closer to
life than others—
purple, the red-blue
heir of a cut.
a bruise greens
when
hemoglobin breaks
down, then yellows.
green nausea
in the dermis.

Nan's Lover Sees the Evidence of His Abuse

after Nan One Month After Being Battered *by Nan Goldin (1984)*

> *Here, Nan is shown beaten by a lover with whom she had an intense sexual relationship. They stayed together even when every other aspect of their connection failed. He almost blinded her in his act.*
>
> *She wears her bruises and bloody eye with almost pride. She withstood it, and she is still here. Her injuries look so severe that we need to look closely. We could almost mistake it for makeup.*
>
> *Her hair is glossy and styled. Her lips bear red lipstick, and her clothing and jewelry suggest she is going out. The violence does not stop her from living her life.*
>
> —Christopher Bryan-Smith, on Nan Goldin's photograph (Expert Photography, 2024)

Nan, you make me
criminal. Lookin' at you
like this, when your lookin'
comes with guilt. I feel like
I done you up real bad,
and you went and dragged
this thing out for almost forty
years when you took this
picture. Nan, I swear I ain't mean
no harm, just wanted
to scare ya, that's all. See,
your lipstick's done, your hair's
all nice, I ain't beat no
pretty up out of ya.
But I could've. Should've, after
you go and pull sum'n

like this. Bitch ain't nobody
gotta know our
business. And who's gon'
believe ya? Could be makeup
for all they know.
And you still so pretty
like I said, how bad could I
have hurt ya? Nan,
baby look at me. I said look
at me. *How bad
could I have hurt ya?*

The Monster You May Marry

on watching the WandaVision *trailer*
after heartbreak

Consider the quotidian horrors—this life your '80s sitcom with a laugh
    track, the audience who knows
how this ends. Your husband, a pomaded perfection. Before he kisses you
    goodbye, you say the thing
you always say. *I'll have dinner when you get back, darling.* The twinkle in his
    eye a gun's misfiring.
You lose your mind a little more every day. Misplace your keys **[Laughter]**
    burn the chicken, we know

how this ends; your husband a pomaded perfection before he kisses you.
    Goodbye. You say the thing
any woman would say, *well, darling, don't you love me?* And he says, *sure I do,*
    honey, flat. **[Laughter]**
You lose your mind a little more. Every day, misplace your keys, laughter.
    Burn the chicken. *We* know
your husband is two-timing, two-stepping into a hotel room lit dim enough
    for imagination, where

any woman would say, *well, darling, don't you love me?* and he says, *sure I do,*
    honey. Flat laughter,
a time stamp we rewind back to catch | to catch | the catch in his voice.
    You're putting on lipstick and
your husband is two-timing. Two-stepping into a hotel room, lit dim
    enough. For imagination, where
do you fold your anguish? In the fitted sheets? **[Laughter]** The lacy lingerie
    still splendid in the
    drawer?

A time stamp we rewind back to catch? To catch the catch in his voice,
  you're putting on lipstick and
freckling your neck with perfume—mussed-up hair, a vision of sex when he
  calls to say *don't wait up.*
Do you fold your anguish in the fitted sheets' laughter? The lacy lingerie still
  splendid in the drawer
mocks you. **[Laughter]** The only thing that will warm you between your
  thighs. Your husband
  returns,

freckling your neck with perfume. Mussed-up hair, a vision of sex. When he
  calls to say *don't wait up,*
you always say, *I'll have dinner when you get back, darling.* The twinkle in his
  eye (a gun's misfiring)
mocks you. Laughter, the only thing that will warm you. Between your
  thighs, your husband returns.
Consider the quotidian; horrors, this life, your '80s sitcom with a laugh
  track, the audience who knows.

Sculpture Study #3

Birmingham, AL

The woman watched the scene from the bathroom doorway: her boyfriend plucking her journal from the nightstand, opening it to a page and mouthing the words she'd written into an old, static-hued morning. In the kitchen; a teakettle howling. There was the potential for two opposite things: love and hate. Between those two things: sex [as her night slip dipped below her left collarbone] and violence [because she was soft enough, her smallness backlit by the bathroom window]. There had been nothing good to report in the journal for months: an inventory of bruises, her new obsession with color. Autopsies of all her little deaths. On his arms, he wore tattoos of his own losses [the date of his mother's passing, his late wife's]. The ink of them now tightens with his anger. *I'll go pour the tea*, she says. The journal tumbles from his fingers, lands open on the carpet—on the opened page, *How do I tell him I don't love him anymore*, in purple, underlined in green and yellow. *The tea, it's ready*, she says, turning to leave as he captures her. His large hand closes around her neck, which could mean anything. *The tea*—cut off by a kiss or slap. It . . . is here that I admit I looked away. The kettle began to whistle. He carried her out of my sight. I'm *telling* you, I'm ashamed. I didn't see a thing.

Tell It Like a Movie | Rewind*

CW/TW: sexual assault, sexual violence

The camera looks away depending on who's behind it. You know the scene:
the woman who has been a woman the whole film now a girl again in a man's
growing

shadow. And the director
makes him larger than even he could imagine himself, but of course, *of course*,
it's just the low-angle shot. And the heels the woman must gasp

out of. Still in her work clothes—the pencil skirt with
seams that will sigh apart in his hands, the button-down, that button the
director needs to pop for *extra effect*, the one that takes ten takes / ten cuts

to get right. The wall the woman backs into
again and again remembers

her shape. Takes her in its own way, holds the warmth of her
backside from every last try, presses like a crotch with demands. But back to
the growing

shadow, how the woman is a girl again plucked

from the safety of flatness, her body's
first curves begging things to tower over her. The camera gets a shot of her
first scream over his shoulder as he closes in, high-angle to mimic girlhood.
The director tells her to put her hands

*up and out, he's gotta have
a clean grab of your shirt collar, up and out.* Down and in on the first three
takes—she can't turn off her instincts. When the grab is right, the director
says her scream isn't real enough, thinks she must imagine her mother

dying to feel grief in this moment.
Tells her *holler like you've just walked in on her, face down, no pulse.* Ten more
takes and nothing. So everyone takes five. And while the woman stamps
her red pout on the rim

of a coffee cup, the director tells the man to
improvise the next take, says *we need surprise on our side, she's gotta feel something.*
And so the director smirks when they return to set, the woman smoothing
her skirt, primping her collar for

crushing. The director yells
Action!, and when the man goes straight for the skirt, it gives. The woman

screams like someone has died—her mother on the bathroom tile, a cold cheek imprinted with small diamonds. And the man keeps pulling

until the woman is standing in the middle of the set in her bra and panties, and he reaches for that too. The director yells *Cut!* And the woman's makeup is ruined. And the director says *that was the emotion we needed, that looked believable.* And the man grins,

satisfied. And the woman finds the torn skirt and wraps it around herself. And she looks into the camera because that's what she's been taught to do, smudged mascara, streaked foundation and all. And the man's belt buckle is

undone. And her lips are cracked from the screaming, so she licks them and is met with salt.

And you are met with salt, licking your lips that are cracked from the screaming, the unbuckled belt,

the man. Streaked foundation, smudged mascara, you look into the camera. Because it's what you've been taught to do, you wrap the torn skirt around yourself. You find the man satisfied, grinning. That looks believable, that is the emotion

we needed. The director says your makeup is ruined, yells *Cut!* And he reaches for you until you stand in the middle of the set in your bra and panties. Your cold cheek imprinted with small diamonds, like the bathroom tile

your mother died on. You scream. And it gives, the skirt. The man thinks, goes straight for the action. Crushes everything—your primped collar, your smooth skirt. The set returns. The director smirks, saying *she's gotta feel*

something, surprise. The next take the man improvises. The director pulls from his coffee cup. You stamp and pout, so everyone takes five. And nothing. Ten more takes. No

pulse, like he's just walked in on you face down. You feel grief, imagine your mother dying, your scream not real enough in that moment. The grab is right. Turn off

your instincts. On the first three takes—down and in, up and out, a clean grab of your shirt collar. The director tells you to put your hands up to mimic

girlhood. High-angle as he closes in,

your scream shot over his shoulder. The camera towers over you, begs
your body's first curves. Safety flattened, plucked from the girl
again. Plucked from the woman. The shadow is back, growing
demands. A crotch presses, tries every last backside, holds
you in it, takes your shape, remembers again and again. You back into a wall
to get ten cuts, ten takes, the one for extra effect. *The button
pops.* The director needs the button-
down in his hands, sighing apart at the seams. The pencil skirt, still work
clothes you must gasp out of. And the heels, low, of course, *of course*. It's just
the angle that makes
him. The director, large again, a man's growing
shadow. The whole film now, the woman who has been a woman—you know
the scene. Behind it, the camera depends on who's looking away.

* In Bernardo Bertolucci's 1972 film, *Last Tango in Paris*, Bertolucci and actor Marlon
Brando decided to use butter in a scripted rape scene without telling the actress,
Maria Schneider. Of the scene, Schneider remarked in 2007, "I was so angry . . . I felt
humiliated and to be honest, I felt a little raped, both by Marlon and by Bertolucci."

Resting Bitch Face

Something about the set of my face says *slave*, cracks sharp in
its stank and slits you uncomfortable. And what do you make
of me again—in that gas station parking lot, in the grocery aisle
and its fluorescence—when you tell me to smile for you? *You too
pretty to be frowning* makes a fugitive of me, shutters me closed
for your business. You even smooth-talk yourself into a lie, say
smile and mean *relax*,

                 mean *open*,

                       mean *peel back*,

                             mean *lights, camera,
action, put on a show for me.* Last time I smiled for a man my
teeth sparked white in the dark of his bedroom like police lights
in a rearview mirror. What could I afford with that currency
besides his violence? Smiling has never bought me tenderness,
never tendered me a love that let my face be bitch, and ain't
that what you gon' call me anyways? Whether I thaw out for
you or not, don't this always end the same—the bright you
coax from my mouth snuffed out as soon as I show it to you?

My Friend Says Steven Spielberg Is Invited to the Cookout

because *The Color Purple gave us too many quotable moments.* In the group chat, we mimic Mister's daddy talking about Shug—*black as tar, legs like baseball bats.* In everyday conversations, my mother seasons her words with parts of Sofia's field speech—*all my life I had to fight*—her black eye plummed up in the sun after Harpo put a fist to it. I learned early on how to juice laughter from the pulp of a collective pain. Years later I read the book and realized that what I didn't get in the movie outweighs what I got, that things are never themselves when you view them through the lens of something else. In the movie, Celie and Shug playfully kiss each other on the bed, and then the record stops playing. In the book, they have sex, fall in love. In the book, Shug leaves but then returns to Celie, desperate as a man who has forgotten his wallet and keys. In the film, Shug leans forward and presses her lips against Celie's, chaste and proper. The camera cuts to their hands moving to the other's shoulder, then pans to a lone wind chime in the open window. What other music did we deserve there? I have not forgiven him for turning our heads.

Are You Jealous | A Burning Haibun
(form created by Torrin A. Greathouse)

after Are You Jealous? *by Paul Gauguin (1892)*

> *It doesn't take a politically minded scholar or*
> *critic to recognize that his representations of nude*
> *Tahitians reflect a sexual and racial fantasy forged*
> *from a position of patriarchal, colonialist power.*
>
> —Meredith Mendelsohn, on Paul Gauguin's
> problematic artistic legacy (Artsy, 2017)

You've caught the sacred side-eye, the purgatory between a woman's interest and disgust. The imprecision of a gaze you've willed your way with instructions—*yes, yes, just like that*—those same instructions I know you cycled through while you doled out a different kind of stroke. You say, *bring your leg up to your chest, yes, look natural.* Try to open her before you open her up. But she knows your kind, denies you the angle she knows you want. In that hot sun, you map out your future explorations—the two mountains of her breasts, the rivulets of her belly creasing against her thigh, the blue sky of her painted toes. The valley between her legs uncharted. You can't paint her legs apart, Paul. What, you angry? Are you jealous? Oh hell, can't you take a joke? I was kidding.

the   purgatory
between a   man's
          gaze   —
                                              instructions
                              doled out
              You say,
                              open
                      But she   denies
              she knows   that
      map

of

You

Paul.   you angry

jealous   hell

yes, yes, just like that—

open her   In that hot sun,

sky of   legs apart

Sculpture Study #4

Cincinnati, OH

One of her earliest kinks—knife play with light, the most unreliable
surgeon. Before the touch of a man, there was heat. Her own
and other; I mean, what she could stoke inside herself
and that external, passive warmth. There is so
much scripture about sunlight because
there's weight behind it; cue
the equations on mass,
the metaphors
about

                    the sun
                    beating

                                on a back.
                         I read somewhere
                    that we first learn tender-
                ness from our mothers, suckling
            at a darkness. That early neediness scored
        from my memory. Instead, I recall myself shifting
     away from the inquisitive sun in the mornings, my body
  split into different fractions as the day came. Even my mother's
first touch asked something of me: a first cry, a toothless maw, a love.

Your Husband Says Let's Try Something New

after The Lovers *by René Magritte (1928)*

after your anniversary dinner, a bit of Bordeaux still aging
on the corner of your mouth. In the restaurant's dim corner he frisked
the top button of your dress undone, its plastic clicking against
the gold wedding band. His hand a half-formed promise counting the dips
of your spine. You offered yourself up right then, plated, drizzled
with need under the table. Your pantyhose, decoration. His fingers
dipped into the chocolate sauce on your plate then paused at your bottom
lip's altar and you wanted to be the pen he signed the check with,
an instrument to do his bidding. At home, he refused to be uncollared,
untied. Left in his cuff links. Said the night was about how far
you could go without going, or coming. Said close your
eyes. A few anniversaries ago you opened a slim jewelry box and found
a leather eye mask slumbering in velvet. *So we can truly be ourselves
in the dark*, as he slid it over your head. His body a new body
in that man-made night—a hunter gone prey to the beast he hoped
you would become. Now, he crowns you with the elastic band
once again, the leather's edge biting a curve into the bridge
of your nose. *Imagine we're both someone else*, he whispers, guiding your hand
to the gill of his boxers. A few seconds of clumsiness, teeth
clicking, the choppy unzipping. Your husband changing shape
in your grip, your name changing shape in the air between
the two of you. *Imagine we're someone else*—as he breathes another
woman's name, asks her for mercy you will not give.

When the Therapist Asks About Intimacy

My silence measures the distance between
now and a memory: the last time a man dug

his thumb into my taut muscle to give me
another pleasure. That same man listened

for God's name as I sat on the floor
between his legs. Above me, he parted my

hair into sections, double-fingered
the grease he would lay in each valley.

Back then, it was the most patient his touch
would ever be. What is it about this that I return

to? That game of following the shadows
that danced at my feet from the candlelight?

His bashful laughter when I praised his
gardening hands? There was no release

waiting for him, nothing straining
like a rubber band in the stretch

before snapping, and he touched me
anyway. But it is always more sinister

than this. *What makes that so intimate?*
the therapist reiterates. I curved my spine

into a man's hands and he did not
kill me. There must have been love.

Eavesdropping

My father talked about me in hushed tones
on the phone. He said I understood him.

On the phone, he said I understood him
when he was drunk, when no one else bothered.

When he was drunk, when no one else bothered
to listen to him, he blew up my phone

to listen. To him, he blew up my phone
because I owed him this therapy.

Because I owed him this, therapy
was complicated. My shame, the blame I took

was complicated. My shame, the blame I took—
old cycles I repeated. The new men like

old cycles I repeated. The new men, like
my father, talked about me in hushed tones.

Made Over

after Goosebumps *by Sally Mann (1990)*

> *In the early 1990s, photographer Sally Mann*
> *transformed one of the most banal elements of*
> *family life—the sentimental photo album—into*
> *discomfiting, divisive, and ultimately unforgettable*
> *artwork. For her series "Immediate Family," she shot*
> *her three children (Emmett, Jessie, and Virginia) in*
> *vulnerable positions at their summer home in rural*
> *Virginia. The ensuing criticism the images received*
> *questioned the line between pornography and fine*
> *art and problematized the objectification of children.*
>
> —Alina Cohen, on Sally Mann's photographs
> of her children (Artsy, 2018)

A mother sees the seed she's planted flexing
toward the sun and wants to remember her
child's singular joy. The girl is a girl forgetting
her girlness, misremembering the churr

of a boy's approval, and shouldn't a mother be proud
of this? The photo tells me the day was hushed
by birdsong. The only word between them: the loud
click of the camera. The daughter's flushed

skin smoothed by a charming sun. Seemingly safe
in her mother's gaze until she multiplied
under the eyes of men. They made a waif
of her, an orphan of her mother's pride.

Her spine, only a place for a man to rest
a hand. The skin as land, the skin as conquest.

"Locker Room Talk" with Satan

after The Fallen Angel *by Alexandre Cabanel (1847)*

I'd ask if it hurt when you fell from heaven but maybe it's too soon for jokes. Hell, you only see the world in opposites—good/bad, God's word/yours. So what was the damage this time, which angel did you imagine as a harp for your plucking? Oh and it's beautiful music, I'd banish myself to hear it. I'd say God knew better than to give me wings, but then again, you held his favor once, didn't you? Thought the man upstairs ain't make mistakes. But son, I could tell by your face it was a woman that did you in. And man, ain't much different down here either. Just like the good book says, was a woman that gave us that fruit, and God knew we'd take a bite out of anything ripe a woman held to our lips. Sounds like a setup if I'd ever heard of one. But you know all about that, don't you, being set up? God knew what you were, still dropped you down in the middle of his prettiest creatures and thought you'd keep your hands to yourself. No, don't tell me how soft she was, I'd prefer to never know. But enough about that. So what's the plan? Your contract is done. Good-looking guy like yourself could have anything he wants, make something of himself around here. And the women? You can grab 'em by whatever you can get a handful of, they're always asking for it, always asking. Come on, let's get you laid. Show God that we got our own commandments. 1. It's all ours for the taking. 2. Every part of a woman is the apple—once you take a bite, you'll learn all there is to know.

Park Proposal (a Chōka)

Down by the fountain,
a man lowers himself down
to one knee. The ring,
a counterfeit sun. I see
the woman process
his silent question, her face
overshot with rage.
Through my eyes' wide sniper scope,
I watch the bullet
of my understanding catch
her shoulder. She stumbles back.

Duplex of Lessons

I discovered the body is a bomb
to be detonated by a gentle touch.

    To be detonated by a gentle touch
    is to give up control, let go of the reigns.

Is to give up control (let go of the reigns)
the only way to test a man's love?

    The only way to test a man's love—
    deny him the flesh. See how long he waits.

Deny him the flesh. See how long he waits
to betray you or blame you for his weakness.

    To betray you or blame you for his weakness—
    what's worse? Is this the reason I'm still alone?

What's worse is this. The reason I'm still alone;
I discovered the body is a bomb.

DRY DOWN

n. • /drī daůn/
a process that occurs when solvents evaporate
from a paint coating, leaving it feeling dry to
the touch
—Charles S. Brown, PaintSquare

Even though a painting may be dry to the
touch, it is not 100 percent dry until cured.

Discomfort at the MoMA

Facing Kazuo Shiraga's *Untitled*, a Black woman considers its red, corpulent layers, how the brushstrokes swirl into a maroon scab in the middle. Nearby, a couple shares an intimate hug in front of *Blue Monochrome* by Yves Klein, breaking the suction between their torsos just enough to kiss long and open by the painting's tense blue field. A guard monitors the calyx of guests moving along the borders of the room. Restless teenagers test how closely they can point at a painting without touching it. A quick white flash from an iPhone camera in the center of the room.

The couple ambles over to another piece of art, not to witness it, but to make it their backdrop. The white man who has just taken a photo on his iPhone switches to video mode, slyly moves the couple into view. The guard takes note of the couple as he moves his hand to his double-breasted jacket, where a walkie-talkie sits, stately and crisp. The Black woman in front of *Untitled* considers if she would feel so strongly about the painting without the texture. Is red ever flat with its violence?

The white man turns off the flash on his iPhone. The couple is making out now, running their tongues along the insides of the other's mouth in front of taxi yellow, eggplant purple. The Black woman takes another step toward *Untitled*, mindful of the book bag she was instructed to mount to the front of her body, acutely aware of the ache swaggering itself into her lower back. The Black guard now, in conversation with the small speaker at his chest.

The Black woman wonders what *Untitled* would be called if it had been named otherwise, contemplates its crime-scene coagulations, is in awe of the disgust skulking in her throat, the vague metallic smell that she knows has no physical source. The white couple continues to monopolize the view of a painting, oblivious to the glares. Forced laughter coils around the room. The Black guard takes a step forward. The white man with the iPhone reduces himself to the recognizable chirp of the record button.

The Black guard is loud in his confrontation on purpose—*I think the decor in your home would be a better audience.* The white man with the iPhone captures the couple's embarrassment in real time, embarrassment that crusts into a rage about public spaces and displays and who can perform for any audience. The Black woman, her back truly aggrieved now, waddles from *Untitled* to *Blue Monochrome* and notes the cooler tension she feels, the endless blue becoming histrionic in her trance. She tries to guess what the white couple felt when they looked, if this lonesome expanse sent them searching, searching for anyone who would see them and say, *look.*

Formal

The distance between this new me and the old
is unmendable. My friends are confounded
by a picture of me from seven years ago; my face hemmed up

by fresh heartache, unastonished
by the boyfriend that held me in the frame
of his suit jacket's sleeves. It was a gala, we made ourselves

anonymous with lace masks
and rhinestones. The backdrop was a hurricane
of triplicate tulle. *You look completely different,*

my friends say, and who doesn't when the lens finally
focuses? Outside of this moment, I was a planet blurred
and spinning around his orbit. He loved me with the clarity

of a drunkard. When the photographer stopped
to take our picture, he arranged us like dolls, my Barbie-
stiff hand pressed to my boyfriend's lapel. I was out

of practice, then, of being gentle after so much
cruelty. I am inexperienced, now, with loving
the version of me that allowed it,

her perpetual existence.

In the War Photography Exhibit, I Find So Many Things Wrong

after Henri Huet's photos of Vietnam War

I do not name a specific exhibit because it doesn't make a difference; in each one it's all the same. I gaze at black-and-white prints of children peeking through the blinds of gritty smoke, just-dead bodies still opening themselves to feed what lives on. And what lives on must gaze into the camera. There is something about capturing the thing looking. Something about permission, being able to say "They saw me take it so where's the harm?" The photographer forgets they lend us their eye in the museum. That in their pictures, they capture more of themselves than the death-ridden landscape. In the war photography exhibit, I look at a picture of a lifeless body ascending toward a helicopter. I know I'm supposed to think that this is something like going to heaven. I also know that there's no God here.

I do not
make a difference;

gritty
opening
into the camera.
There is   the
permission   to
harm
forget
capture
the death-ridden
exhibit,   a   body
I'm supposed
to
know

name a   difference   each
photographer forgets   .   the
body   is *something*

One of Many

You're naked in our bed, harp-tight from the cold I require to sleep deeply. Your phone on the nightstand, and the light from a notification opens into the room like a book.[1] I undress in my dark corner. I rustle around like something paranormal and harmless. Each piece of clothing huffs into a pile at my feet. After all this time, I still believe I don't have to ask you for anything. You call this role-play—how you slide up toward the headboard and pose like a monarch. The way a body's posture can ask the right question. I slink across the room to the tune of your phone vibrating again.[2] The caller haunts this sacred moment and you smirk in the apparition's Technicolor white. Role-play is a euphemism for how I abandon myself to be seen by you. This is an audition tape*rewind*we will have sex as if we are alone now but someone will watch it back later*rewind*your mind is on the other end of a landline while you talk me through it. How you can be here and gone, split in two—true *pornography, role-play, performance.* Me: a star in one of your many films. We callous in the cold. I rake my fingers through the black-haired cityscape erected south of your navel. Someone is calling again.[3] If I have a name, you can't remember it.

---

1 **Voicemail**: *Hey babe, I texted earlier, you good? Was checking on you and seeing if we still good for this weekend. I checked the prices on the rental car, look like the SUV will be cheaper. You cool taking most of the driv—*

2 **Voicemail**: *My bad, I hung up on the last one. But why you not picking up? I need you to pick my lingerie set, check your messages! Aight bye.*

3 **Voicemail**: *One more thing, one more thing. I want you to do that thing I like. [Laughter] You coming over tonight? Damn, where you at? I miss you.*

Well Damn, Picasso

after The Red Armchair *by Pablo Picasso (1931)*

> *He submitted them to his animal sexuality, tamed*
> *them, bewitched them, ingested them, and crushed*
> *them onto his canvas. After he had spent many*
> *nights extracting their essence, once they were bled*
> *dry, he would dispose of them.*
>
> —Marina Picasso, on her grandfather
> Pablo Picasso's treatment of women
> (*Picasso: My Grandfather,* 2001)

By the looks of her, she's near the end of your need.
A palimpsest of textures, fabrics, a bust
you busted down to static, curves you three-d
like fractures, the simple geometry of her body trussed

to the chair like nothing separate from it—the math
of your control. Picasso, she's so scared
she doesn't know which way to look, and you're mad
enough to show it and make her two-faced. Dared

to glam her up in the color of bruises and hope
we wouldn't notice. Right there, the muscadine
of how she hurts. Pablo, I see the blood by the slope
of her bangs, in the pink of her cheeks. It's easy to find

your hunger. Dammit Pablo, nobody taught
you you could love a thing you hadn't caught?

Sonnet for Longing Being Mistaken for Sadness

Honey, the sun's no longer centrifugal.
For weeks, its yellow failed to pull me
out of unliving; the hip-dug dip my usual
position leaves in bed. I lie here, fully

naked, unsexed. The only remnants of life—
the tetris of take-out boxes castling around
the nightstand, noodles dried and circling a knife
like legs, and again, the honey-thickened sound

of lonely. Even the doctor is bodiless,
a pixelated ghost who can't prescribe
me what I need—a hand to pull me out of this
by my thighs, and *oh*, an epiphany. I transcribe

alone as *unloved*. I touch myself, then don't.
I will a man to call, knowing he won't.

The Ocean as Misogynist

I sit where the sand is dark with
wet. When the tide comes
in, it begs like a man
I've already said no to, grows
hungrier. First it laps
at my ankles, then lips
my thighs. Finally the tide circles
my waist before retreating.
I finger the word "no"
in the muck. The water erases
it, makes me write it over and over.

The Violence of Rain

after Truong Tran

a man. told me. to shut up. and i. obeyed. i still haven't. forgiven myself. for
letting my silence. be on his time. his dime. paid for my submission. he paid.
every bill. in the house. i paid. for my hair. for my nails. for not knowing.
better. we argued. about money. i was worried. about where. he spent it.
instead of. who. he spent it. on. that day. rage. rented a space. within me. then
rented my lips. apart. i said. *money does not keep you. home.* i said. *you green.
then gone.* i said. *you splitting. bills. in hotels. bills. on the nightstand. bills. paid
late. the lights. off. the lights. cut off.* i said. *i'm not paying. for shit.* you butted. in.
butted your forehead. against. mine. your lips. kiss-close. said. *shut. the fuck
up.* that was the first. time. you told me. the last time. you had to. i shut. down.
shut. up. i shut. the fucking. out. i didn't let you. fuck. me. again. you. fucked.
off. fucked. outside. our house. like the animal. you were. i was so. quiet. in
everything. i said. i was. a whisper. i was. wind. tornado. forming. in your
face. i looked. still. because i was. coming. toward. you. you. said. *shut. the
fuck. up.* and i. was rain. how you. can only. hear it. when. it strikes. something.
how. it punctuates. is. a period. splintering. into. more.

Applied Theory

One could argue it's all about perspective. Or speed.
Like the coal mine rolling upward to greet me
as I drove back into Ohio from Pittsburgh, twisted muscle/
machine shining in the sun. I rode by so fast
I misrecognized it at first, saw the prelude
of a water park peeking above the hill's edge. A trick built in
by a man's design—to appear harmless
in the beginning—the glittering mine not yet a nightmare
or monster hoarding moonlight in his knife.

One could also make the argument for angles. At the top
of the hill, I slowed to ten below the limit. I could fully look down
on the mine and feel what it was like to pass
judgment. I saw its secrets, or the secrets of its creator
because it too is made in the image of its God. And again,
everything suggesting innocence. The great silos
like cookie tins neatly stacked, the raw coal breaker
like a small house whose only crime was
its poor design. The antagonistic turns
of the tunnels. What do they say?—*lacking a woman's touch.*

I would like to make a case for surveillance. A theory
of stillness and looking long enough to see
the way men build *through* things. Squinting in sunlight
to catch the gouged mountainside. More violence
below the drilling. In observation lies
a translation.

I test this theory on my relationship, and it seems
that testing love is the only way to dig into
its true form. I was in love with a man
and one day I became still. In the mornings. While he talked.
In his noise. When he stormed out. I watched
and stopped scurrying to fill our every beat
with offering. I looked down on him and what had glittered became
ordinary. Dull. In my mind, he had been blurred
and beautiful from all my movement. I see it now, the love
I loved was my own. Translation:
I gave him color.

Girls' Night

On scary movie night, I called in company. My girl friend's arrival was the first jump scare, her silhouette hunched in my front door's frosted glass before she rang the bell. In her hand, a gift of red wine. The movie we picked was arbitrary, I couldn't stop watching her. And this isn't about a blossoming love or attraction, but fear. Changing weather. The overcast living room and the two of us in murderous light. The thing is, she was the closest to being a man than she'd ever been, relishing in the gore. Sometimes there is no line between awe and arousal, I witnessed it then: her shallow breathing, her dilated eyes as the killer crept a knife along his victim's collarbone. Again, these blurred lines between dissonant things. As the killer made his first cut, my friend leaned forward, and spilled red onto the carpet. The victim's gasp and her gasp the same gasp. Pain and pleasure, perhaps not so different. She watched the killer and all his flourish while I watched her: pitched forward, hungry like a madman, or maybe like a husband watching his wife on the edge of their bed, opening herself. Her insides dripping onto the floor.

I'm Trying to Tell You Something

The opening shot places me in an old boyfriend's kitchen. [Alien cleanliness of a furniture showroom. A window, perfectly placed, through which the sunlight accordions across the granite. A dripping dish towel noosed around the faucet's spout. The silence so absurd that it mutes the expected plop against the stainless steel.] I am an interruption on this set, standing in front of the full sink of dishes before stopping the drain. Something robotic in my movements. Then, a close-up of my face, the running dishwater hazing into a fecal brown in my eye's mirror. [Over that sound, a separate human sound from upstairs, too regular for sex, and so maybe snoring, an unfortunate angling of pillow.] This is how memory comes to me; like the nasal-edged static of *911, what's your emergency*, how it grates even when you're the one that made the call. At the sink, a choice has to be made. I can't see through the water. I left the sharp knives in and I want to know them, again, better this time around. *911, what's your emergency?*—I am in need of some other answer than the one I have. There's a bird's-eye shot over my head, directly into the sink. As the water rises, a few bowls bob to the surface, streaked with abstract remainders of mush. If there is art to be found here, I am the gallerist, I'm trying to show you something then sell it. A shadow gathers behind me, the old boyfriend pressing that the dishes must be clean before the guests arrive. I plunge my right hand into the deep. *911, what's your emergency?* Familiar warmth. A slow, menstrual bleed under the water.

Sonnet for My Dating Life

Three of my handmade paintings hang in a man's
loft here in Cincinnati, all of which he watched
me paint in real time. It was like sex—my hands
wettened, the delicate wristwork, my body splotched

with fingered accidents. I used to wonder
about the difference between pastoral works
and portraiture—the same approach to under-
standing a place, versus a face. It hurts

to remember how he watched me with an artist's
eye on the floor in my apartment, how
his looking was bullied by want. Desire, the sharpest
elastic snap from person to landscape. Now

I know I was both. We never kissed. I touched
his face. There's excerpts of me on his wall, collecting dust.

A Valentine's Day Poem to Myself at 25

I know you too well, how you long
for everything that chafes against your
history. I watch you order yourself
a bottle of wine, a steak greased
in garlic butter. See you buy yourself
new lingerie and still wish for another
mouth to remove it, the remnants
of a barrel-mouthed man stuck to
the edges of you loving yourself. Girl,
who you foolin'? I know the temptation
to perform for what ain't there. To hip into
that garter belt like someone is watching
from the doorway, humming
their approval for the way that red lifts
your ass in offering. To set up
your camera, turn on the timer, and
imagine its shutter clicks as the clucks
of a lover's tongue before he details
all the ways he'll unwrap you. All these years
and you never learned to fully taste
anything; all the notes in a glass of wine,
yourself. Got all those mirrors
in your bedroom and ain't practiced
a thing. You are *yours*, your own
body to teach again how to heed
a hand, and whose. Been so long that you
forgot the sound of your own name.
In that mirror, call yourself to your own
heat, to your own junction between
your thighs. Look yourself in the eyes and know
that you can love yourself if just so *you*
can watch from the door, if only to look
damn good while doing it. Say your name.
Can't nobody say it like you anyway.

Re-narrativization

We all know what vultures do near the dying or already dead, their slow unfolding into umbrellas of dark. In the sky, a carouseled caution for the coming feast. So what does it mean when they follow me home? Yes, a funeral trucks me toward Chicago. A funeral is already in my mind. But death isn't on me yet. Or it is, and the birds belt a bracelet overhead because they know what I don't. There's extra vibration in my steering wheel, the thread in my tires worn down. There is the bird's language and then there is mine, different systems of symbols. I choose to rename this foreshadowing, call their vague choreography a halo. I see the slit between sky and ground and claim another year of this life instead of heaven. I drive through it. I will be home soon. The birds, so predictable, scatter at my declaration of permanence.

Love Poem, Attempt 1/?

On FaceTime calls, my mother finger-taps the side of her head
when the truth occurs to her. And it is always arriving again
when we speak.

Last week, I called my mother from bed, and she caught
the bed restraints on my headboard in the frame. We laughed
and released our different truths—she called me a *freaky girl* while

I admitted I'd never used them. Sometimes we collide
like that, our revelations canceling each other out. Tonight, I invite
my mother to cry with me—neither of our faces on camera,

just the intimacy of us visiting our shared, imprisoned
sadness. Our loneliness, ornate and parading as other things,
like hunger, or our constant calls to the other. Our gospels bustle

through the night. My mother says, *I just want companionship, but I don't
trust anyone after the divorce.* I think of the man I love, how he loves me too
but loves me less, and send a fact back: *Sometimes love doesn't look the way*

I want it to, but it's still the love I need. My mother marvels
at our differences, her finger drumming the soft bowl of her temple.
Her confusion becoming legible, askable—*but aren't you wasting*

your time loving a man who hasn't chosen you? And again, we crash
about definitions of love: hers singular in shape and size, mine fluid
and slippery. But then she's laughing again, remembering:

You're right-brained and I'm left-brained, that's why we love so differently.
What she means is that she loves in black and white, and I love in the gray
area, that she is all or nothing, and I have learned to enjoy a good thing

while it lasts. Each of us, surviving this same world antithetically.
We do what we have to do, I say, wrapping my arms around myself.
In Chicago, in my mother's bedroom, the truth arrives in the same

gesture, unknowingly, my touch becoming her touch, and becoming
mine again as she hugs me in her head. Between us, a silent certainty
chugging through static—we are always holding each other in the dark.

In a Past Life

It is easy to get turned around
in this world, to fall asleep in one place and wake
eyeing down the revolver of a forgotten
room. I ask a friend, *does this ever happen*
to you? and she says disorientation is really a moment
of clarity, me switchblading
into a past life. The time between different lives
doesn't stretch, but darkens. The time between now
and where I slip to sometimes, bruise-blue.
Yesterday, I felt compelled to stand out in the rain and be
anchored by it. Fresh brushstrokes
in my eyes, watercolor of wet mascara.
I blinked but couldn't holster the gun, the old world
peeking through. The path home foreign,
the street names unreadable in the downpour. The stranger
on the other sidewalk turns suddenly,
says a name not mine and yet I knew it was. His face,
a face I briefly remembered to be yours
once. Yes, you can vault from one nightmare
into another—I am the arrowhead that strokes through
forgetting, remembering, then forgetting again.

Evidence

after photographs by Adeolu Osibodu

You strip through the lake water. You, a smooth fin
in the deep, a lone canoe of muscle. The path
between us, carved out, then flooded

with water replacing itself. I am not
a swimmer, but I can fix a trick of light
with your phone's camera. So I sit in the near-

shore and command the setting sun
with my fingertip. We'd been fighting before
this, on the drive up, about negligence. A lack

of attention. How a scar from ACL surgery
stretched and silvered with my new
weight, how you hadn't kissed the spot

behind my knee in months. As the truck jolted
through the dirt path, my anger rattled,
wounded, in the cab, then bruised

into an embarrassment. When was the last
time I'd poked and prodded
your tattoos in the name of tender

curiosity? Wordlessly, you left me
in the shallow, swam far out to let off
steam. I hold your phone carefully above

the water, take photos of the wet crystals
sliding from your brown skin, the stitches
of your closed eyes when you erupt

from the surface. I see you, an umbra in slick
coral, eloping from our shared hurt.
I want proof, this time, of how I study you.

A Light

Before this, I didn't know loneliness could be toggled. Yesterday, it was an accordion expanding between my own hands, then collapsing when I forced out its song. My loneliness sang the air cyan—that last shade of blue before its final green changeover—sang the air the shade of a mouth filling with saliva before vomiting. And then today, on a road trip by myself, no room for my loneliness among the silence I fashioned from the road's resolute hum. It was nighttime when I arrived in the city, its bisque glow fuzzed over by rain. Dark pants and stockings scuttling under darker, veined parabolas. At a red light, I counted the windows on a glass building, counted upward until the squares softened into sky-fog. On the twelfth floor of the building's black-out, a lone lamp quivered on like an oven door opening. I pictured a man in his bedroom, restless in the consequences of a grave mistake. His crisp sheets mellowed by sweat. Or a woman turning on the bedside light and saying *honey, can you*—turning over toward the answer of a forgotten absence.

Sculpture Study #5

Chicago, IL

The last time I watched its time lapse, the sunset was a slow and steady
ambering. A fire waxed
        flat to the razored grass. And haven't all my lessons about fire bristled

across the sky? I knew the word "fire" before I knew the colors that made it.
Knew its loyalty, the daily sear,

the nightly put-out. Learned quickly that it didn't

        discriminate. The first Fourth of July that I remember, I stood next
to one of many cars parked like tally marks in an open field. Before a fireworks
display, rows of brake lights

        neoned the grass. When the rocket sliced upward and away from me,
I felt safe. By now, I'd also known that heat had to come close to be felt—that
fire whispered

        its confrontation.

        Then the boom came. When the string of light fractured outward,
when the explosion arched

        down and fell back toward the earth, I watched it approach

in terror. Like all things dangerous, here was a flame that reached for me

        with its fingers. Like all things cowardly, here was a flame that waited

        until it was inches away from my face

        to disappear.

Sculpture Study #6, or How Can I Write About Flowers at a Time Like This

after Hanif Abdurraqib

with that green smell of rain in the air, everything binate

in glistening asphalt? Here, in the Walmart parking lot, car tires slash

through puddles in prayer, and God answers

in his gaudy way. My mother's calling inside my

purse, but I dance in the shadow of the store sign that couldn't endure.

I hate how I understand that giving up. Six planets in retrograde

and me, a lone top spinning to someone's subdued music. My shoe

needs to be tied. The laces drag through the wet and whip

arches into the night's back. I should tell you now, I'm losing

my mind, that a buzzing has started in my ears. Small at first, then

like something crawling upward from a grave.

My pillow heavy with it, synonymous to a cloud pregnant

with water; or is this another way of being haunted

by what I've never had? I come here at night for a different quiet:

the couple in the back of the lot, their moans drowned

by the car's horsey idle. The mundane arguments, the husband studying his wife's grocery list in the about-dark, the swish

of my sneakers turning. Then me, dizzy, tumbling—

falling toward myself, blurry. Glitching on the other side.

Ekphrasis on Memory

Your half-eaten apple on the night-
stand: the still life I return to. The triumvirate
of targets from your teeth. Everything
you touched, you touched
brutally. In bed, you bit me like you meant to
grave a crater in the wake of your
suckling. So proud of the pink parentheses
toning down on my breasts. I told you
to stop once, when it was the tender part
of the month and they hurt
to touch. You bit again, harder, laughing,
pressing me into your face. How jealous I become
of the apple in my memory's eye—bitten,
yes, but left alone. Cherished now.

A Grammar of Loneliness

There is the moment when rain heavies into one unending ring, the sky a dark
curtain pulled shut. The clouds, weak as a bladder. Solitude is always messy—the
windowsill peppered wet,

        the thunder outside running a slip knife along the edges of
my sadness, jimmying it open.

        There is a moment when my aloneness
is flayed down to something animal, the bullish man in my mind for years. My
body still capable of rising to a cold wind or warm hand. I'm sorry,

        where are my
        manners?
Language programs a scene in our minds even when we write around it—the
cold wind becomes a goosefleshed nipple, a warm hand dips between the thighs.
I am lonelier here, on the page,

        than I've ever been. While the storm still
drums, I slink out of bed. I find a day's-old bruise in the shower curtain's dark blue
eclipse and massage it. Can I write in tenderness, months later, where it colors

        itself purple?
Where it sleeks itself pink? I could touch myself in the downpour, just like this,
and loneliness will become

a character in the room. And when it makes itself known, I will call it

        by another name.

Poem in Which I Try to Have the Last Word

1.

Men have crueled love out of my language—yes, I still have the voicemails. Now I listen more to their backgrounds: the soundtrack of rain grousing against a car window, a friendly waitress ambiguous in her offerings, *Can I get you anything else?* A man's ego is so large he breaks my heart while talking to himself, chases his voice the way a dog hunts his own tail. Through the tunnel of static, one barely suppresses the glee of cutting a thing deep enough the blood gets greedy for the knife. Another laughs, falls in love with himself. *I just need to focus on me, you know?* He pulls down his visor in the car, parked after a work shift, before a date. He watches himself triple in the eyes of the mirror, feels like some kind of god.

2.

How inconsequential I was, dialed in these transitory moments. On accident from a jean pocket twice—something divine in that. How they called with news as heavy as death, their relief leaking through like water damage. I heard it pooling, darkening into a shapeless puddle on a bathroom ceiling. In one ear, a man broke up with me without me. In the other, I mistook the sound of a leaky faucet as lost love drizzling into an empty tub.

3.

Hi, this is Taylor. I'm sorry I can't answer the phone right now—*Hi, you've reached Taylor*—and this was truer than I knew. A past version of me apologizes for being out of reach because she hasn't learned how sound trebles into sensation. A man's rough hands. *I'm currently unavailable, but if you'll leave your name and number*—I'll remember. It was about power, about a voice lassoing my wrist through the phone just as I turn to leave. Saying *don't go*, having already left.

4.

Even my iPhone tries to save me, the voicemail transcript censoring their last words. *Look, I know you wanted to talk in person, but I feel like this is* ___ (best) (better) (easier) (it) (all I can afford). I play Mad Libs with the messages before I listen. *I think we've just been* _____ *apart* (drifting) (falling) (fucking). *I'll be over to pick up the last of my* _____ *tomorrow* (clothes) (spit). *Just let me know when you'll be* _____ (gone) (at work) (over it).

5.

Hi, this is Taylor, I'm sorry I can't answer the phone right now. But if you'll leave your name and number I'll get back to you as soon as possible. Thank you.

Hi, ▆▆▆▆▆ *I'm sorry I can't* ▆▆▆▆▆▆ *right now.* ▆▆▆▆▆▆▆

Hi, ▆▆▆▆▆▆ *I can't* ▆▆▆▆▆▆▆▆▆▆ *leave* ▆▆▆▆▆▆▆▆▆ *you.*

Hi, this is ▆▆▆▆ *sorry* ▆▆▆▆▆▆▆▆▆▆
▆▆▆▆▆▆▆▆▆▆ .

Hi, this is Taylor, ▆▆▆▆▆▆▆▆▆▆ *if you* ▆ *leave* ▆▆▆▆▆▆ *I'll get back to you* ▆▆▆▆▆▆▆ .

Hi, ▆▆▆▆▆ *I'm sorry I can't answer* ▆▆▆▆
your name ▆▆▆▆▆▆▆▆▆ .

Hi, ▆▆▆ *Taylor, I'm sorry* ▆▆▆▆▆▆▆▆ *But*
▆▆▆▆▆▆▆▆▆▆ .

Hi, ████ *Taylor,* ███████████████████████████████████████ *leave*
████████████████████████████████ *as soon as possible* ████████ .

Hi, this is Taylor, ████████████████████████████ *But if you* ██ *leave*
████████████ *I'll* ██████████████████ *Thank you.*

SIGNATURE

n. • /ˈsig-nə-chŭr/
a person's name written in a distinctive way as a
form of identification
—Oxford English Dictionary

On a painting, a signature can signal that the
work is complete, authentic, and ready to be
released for public consumption.

In the Lens of Desire

after Untitled (Man and Mirror) *from* Kitchen Table Series *by*
  Carrie Mae Weems *(1990)*
after Good Dress *by Brittany Rogers*

I want to be straight-backed and brazen—no, I want to know
that I deserve it. I want a man as quiet as a rumor hovering
over my shoulder. I want a table pebbled with my living and mine
only, his drink drained from my cup. I want the ornery praise

of a good-as-gone Camel's fizzle, bowed in my good glass ashtray.
I want the silk kimono and the camisole, the unsanctioned
nipple and its silhouette showing. I want to stop
wanting, so give me a mirror, a camera, give me my face

in the third silver of a man's eye. Give me a finger that fishhooks
in the corner of my smirk, that crooks a man to my kitchen
when no dinner has been served. Give me a cheekbone sure
as a scar. My new brush, my good comb. Give me hair

so nice it appears twice: *here* and *there*. A photograph in which
I am the center. Give me your eye; I've already given you mine.

Acknowledgments

To have the courage and strength to write a second book after the first required more than anything I could conjure from within. This book only exists because of my incredible community, because of loved ones, mentors, peers, editors, etc. who kept me alive and believed in my work even when I didn't. Endless gratitude to the following individuals and entities:

My two siblings, Jared and Alexis, for always supporting me and letting me be my truest self. To my mother, for sticking by my side no matter the challenges, for loving me and cheering me on, for helping me believe that I deserve this life. To my grandmother, my aunt Devin, and my uncle Dante, for the extra wind under my wings, especially these past few years.

My dearest poet friends, first readers, thought provokers, accountability partners—Seamus Fey, Jason B. Crawford, Dior J. Stephens, Kay Bancroft—for challenging me to be the best version of myself both on and off the page. Our conversations bring me closer and closer to my vision, and by extension, closer and closer to myself.

My dear friends who don't obsess over poems but still celebrate mine endlessly—JeTaun Hyatt, Destiny Hunter, Samantha Shelley, the entire Studio 310 crew—and my dear friends who write other things besides poems and still hype mine up—Hugh Hunter and Megan Pillow—thank you for helping to keep me grounded in this world, for showing me where the joy lives when it seems so hard to find.

My incredible dissertation committee—Dr. Rebecca Lindenberg, Dr. Sharrell Luckett, and Dr. Lisa Hogeland—who helped usher the first version of this book into the world. Your deep engagement with the work (and your questions during my defense) gave me the tools to see the book through its necessary evolutions.

My previous agent, Rena Rossner, for being a part of this book's birth and journey.

Soft Skull Press, for continuing to nurture my work, for your unrelenting excitement for this project, and for your continued hard work for this book. I feel so seen and cared for in your hands, and I believe my book will get the best possible chance on the shelves because of everything you've done and continue to do.

Mensah Demary and Cecilia Flores for being some of the first believers in this book, for the editorial care, for everything.

My poetic heroes, the Black women poets who came before me and made this book possible, the shining North stars that I follow with every poem I write.

My writing community, all the readers, bookstores, universities, festivals, libraries, etc. who have given my work a chance. Thank you for your time, your engagement, for welcoming me into your spaces and sharing my work in your communities. You help make my dreams come true.

The editors, publications, and organizations who gave many of these poems their first light—*Frontier Poetry, Beloit Poetry Journal, Poet Lore, Hooligan Magazine, Big Lucks, Southeast Review, Pigeon Pages, Honey Literary, Split Lip Magazine, Transition Magazine, Winning Writers, Superstition Review, The Journal, New Ohio Review,* and the Taft Museum of Art.

01 14

J

TAYLOR BYAS is an award-winning poet and a Black Chicago native currently living in Cincinnati, Ohio. Her poetry collection *I Done Clicked My Heels Three Times* won the Maya Angelou Book Award, the Ohioana Book Award, the CHIRBy Award, and the BCALA Best Poetry Honor. Find out more at taylorbyas.com.